BECOMING NAOMI LEÓN

by
Pam Muñoz Ryan

Teacher Guide

Written by
Linda Herman

Note

The 2005 Scholastic, Inc., paperback edition of the novel, © 2004 by Pam Muñoz Ryan, was used to prepare this guide. The page references may differ in other editions. Novel ISBN: 0-439-26997-0

Please note: This novel deals with sensitive, mature issues. Parts may contain profanity, sexual references, and/or descriptions of violence. Please assess the appropriateness of this book for the age level and maturity of your students prior to reading and discussing it with them.

ISBN: 978-1-56137-068-9

Printed in the United States of America.

To order, contact your local school supply store, or—

Novel Units, Inc.
P.O. Box 97
Bulverde, TX 78163-0097

Web site: www.novelunits.com

Table of Contents

Skills and Strategies

Comprehension
Creative thinking, identifying attributes, supporting judgments, inference, prediction

Literary Elements
Story mapping, characterization, setting, conflict, theme, symbolism, author's purpose

Vocabulary
Classifying, root words, definitions, homophones, target words

Listening/Speaking
Discussion, debate, interviewing, oral presentation

Writing
Creative writing, narrative, letters, dialogue, speech, journalism, poetry

Critical Thinking
Brainstorming, research, compare/contrast, fact/opinion, cause/effect, analysis, evaluation

Across the Curriculum
Social Studies—Mexican culture, family relationships, bullies, time line, recipes; Science—hummingbirds, potato maze, weather, Mexican redknee tarantula, sea turtles, earthquake preparedness; Health—psychology, positive thinking, nutrition; Art—illustration, design, Mexican folk art; Geography—maps; Music; Math

Genre: fiction

Setting: trailer park in present-day Lemon Tree, California; Oaxaca City, Mexico

Point of View: first person

Themes: non-traditional families, family relationships, physical disabilities, bicultural heritage, fitting in, abandonment, courage, triumph over adversity, discovering one's self

Conflict: person vs. person, person vs. self, person vs. society

Style: narrative

Tone: conversational, candid

Date of First Publication: 2004

Summary

Becoming Naomi León is a story about fifth grader Naomi Soledad León Outlaw's journey to discover the person she is meant to be. Naomi and her younger brother, Owen, live in a California trailer park with their great-grandmother, whom they call "Gram." With the help of Gram's love and positive thinking, Naomi and Owen overcome problems from their past—namely, the trauma of being abandoned by their mother seven years earlier. To Naomi and Owen's dismay, their mother returns, bringing with her a history of alcohol abuse and Clive, her self-centered boyfriend. Naomi and Owen are hopeful about the possibility of a relationship with their newfound mother until they learn of her true intentions to take Naomi to Las Vegas and leave Owen behind. To protect the children, Gram takes them to Oaxaca, Mexico, to search for their father. Naomi discovers the Mexican half of her heritage, her identity, and the courage to help keep her family together.

About the Author

Pam Muñoz Ryan grew up in California's San Joaquin Valley with her two sisters and extended family, including 23 cousins. Like her character Naomi, Ryan has quirky habits and a mixed cultural background. She considers herself "truly American" due to her mixed heritage, composed of Spanish, Mexican, Basque, Italian, and Oklahoman ancestry. "Many American children share a heritage from another country with no knowledge of that country," Ryan says. Unlike Naomi, Ryan speaks Spanish and knows about her heritage.

After college, Ryan worked as a bilingual Head Start teacher and administrator. It wasn't until after she went back to San Diego State University to get a master's degree in education that a colleague encouraged her to write professionally.

Ryan's books for young people include award-winning titles such as *Esperanza Rising, Riding Freedom, Amelia and Eleanor Go for a Ride,* and *When Marian Sang. Becoming Naomi León* has also won awards, including the 2006 Pura Belpré Honor Book and the 2004 Américas Award Commended Title. Some of Ryan's books have been translated into Spanish, and she also writes for a Japanese publisher. "Changing formats and genres, between picture books and novels, fiction and nonfiction, keeps me enthusiastic and challenged," Ryan says. Today, she lives in north San Diego County with her husband, four children, and two dogs.

Background Information

According to Ryan, ideas for her stories are sometimes like a confluence of rivers, as with *Becoming Naomi León*. After finding a book at the airport that mentioned *La Noche de los Rábanos*, the Night of the Radishes, a festival held annually in Oaxaca City, Mexico, Ryan says, "The event sounded so magical I knew I had to see it." In 1997, she traveled to Oaxaca City to attend the festival and returned knowing she had to write about it. Months later, she signed an autograph for a fan named Naomi Outlaw and wondered how the name had affected the girl. Ryan combined those incidents with personal knowledge and research on grandparents who raise their grandchildren. She was startled to learn that statistics show "one in ten children in the U.S. are raised by family members other than their parents, and it's usually the grandparents and often only the grandmother."

Characters

Naomi Soledad León Outlaw: fifth-grade girl; suffers from elective mutism and usually refuses to speak; list maker; soap carver

Owen Soledad León Outlaw: second-grade boy; physically disabled; wears tape on his clothes for comfort; bright and intelligent; maintains a positive outlook

Gram (Mary/María Outlaw): Naomi and Owen's great-grandmother and guardian; loving, positive thinker, and believes in her "Oklahoma notions"

Bernardo and Fabiola Morales: neighbors and "almost kin" to Naomi and Owen; from Oaxaca, Mexico; Bernardo is a woodworker and cares for the avocado grove; Fabiola works on sewing alterations with Gram

Mrs. Maloney: 88-year-old neighbor; opinionated

Ms. Morimoto: Naomi's teacher; popular

Mr. Marble: school librarian; "absolute best person at Buena Vista Elementary"

Skyla Jones (Terri Lynn): Naomi and Owen's mother; abandoned Naomi and Owen and left them with Gram seven years ago; alcoholic; selfish and abusive

Clive: Skyla's boyfriend; tattoo artist; self-centered; renamed his daughter, Elizabeth, "Sapphire"

Blanca Paloma: Naomi's new classmate and friend; talkative

Dustin Mullholler: school bully

Flora and Pedro Martínez: Fabiola's sister and brother-in-law; live in Mexico

Graciela: Flora and Pedro's daughter; doctor's assistant; lives with her parents

Rubén: Graciela's seven-year-old son; Owen's friend

Teresa: Naomi's great-aunt; lives in Mexico; paints Santiago's carvings

Beni Morales: Bernardo's cousin; a carver; lives in Mexico

Santiago Zamora León: Naomi and Owen's father; lives in Mexico; fisherman and carver; good and kind

Judge: presides over Naomi and Owen's custody case

Initiating Activities

1. Predictions: Have students examine the book's cover. Hold a class discussion in which students brainstorm answers to the following questions: Who do you think are the main characters in the novel? What do you think the novel is about? Where/when do you think the novel takes place? Instruct students to read the Using Predictions instructions on page 24 of this guide. Then have students begin the Prediction Chart on page 25 of this guide.
2. Creative Writing/Social Studies: Discuss with students the meaning of non-traditional families. Have students write two or three paragraphs in which they discuss their opinions on the following topics: Can a non-relative be a good parent? What characteristics describe a good parent?
3. Brainstorming/Art: Discuss with students the meaning of identity. Have students brainstorm how each of the following shape who they are: time, place, events, gender, culture, and family. Have students use classroom materials such as markers, colored pencils, etc. to decorate paper bags that symbolize who they are. Tell students they may also use words and pictures from magazines and/or newspapers to decorate their bags if they wish. As a class, view each bag. Have students try to guess the owner of each bag. Then allow the rightful owner to explain the symbols he/she chose.
4. Comprehension: Read aloud "A Clutch of Collective Nouns" at the end of the novel, and have students complete the identification activity given.
5. Art: Read aloud Naomi's list "Things I Am Good At" on the back cover of the novel. Have students create bookmarks that illustrate things they are good at.

Vocabulary Activities

1. Vocabulary Posters: Have students search in magazines and/or newspapers for pictures and words related to collective nouns, including those found in the novel's table of contents. Have students tape, paste, or pin their findings to posters for display in class.
2. Root Word Meanings: Have students find the root words in each of the following vocabulary words from the novel: predisposition, recollection, orthopedics, guardianship, recognition, rehabilitation. Instruct students to answer the following questions for each of the given words on a separate sheet of paper: What is the meaning of the root word? What is the meaning of the prefix or suffix added to the root word? What is the meaning of the vocabulary word? How does the root word's meaning change?
3. Vocabulary Pantomime: Select two or three students to act out, without speaking, the following vocabulary words from the novel: bedraggled, wriggling, plaited, dredge, toting, contorted. Instruct the rest of the class to guess the vocabulary word being acted out.
4. Homophones: List the following pairs of homophones on the bulletin board: weather/whether, peaked/peeked, minor/miner, patients/patience, flour/flower, poured/pored. Instruct students to write one sentence for each word. Sentences should show the different meanings of each homophone.
5. Target Word Definition: Have students create definitions for the following vocabulary words from the novel: whorl, dervish, cattywampus, cornucopias, caterwaul, copal. Encourage students to be humorous in their definitions, but do not allow them to look up any of the words in a dictionary. Read the made-up definitions aloud, and then give the real definition. You may want students to vote for the best made-up definitions (e.g., most accurate or silliest) before giving the correct answer.

a rabble of yesterdays–Chapter 2

Naomi Soledad León Outlaw and her brother, Owen, live with Gram at Avocado Acres Trailer Rancho. Gram uses practical solutions, her "Oklahoma notions," and positive thinking to help her great-grandchildren overcome problems from their past—traumas the children are too young to fully remember or understand. Though Owen has physical disabilities, he is a bright student who believes in luck. Naomi doesn't talk much, but her soap carving and list making keep her mind and hands busy. To Naomi, her biggest problem in life is her name. But that all changes when Naomi and Owen's mother returns after seven long years, saying it's time she gets to know her children.

Vocabulary

unravel
bedraggled
avocado
polyester
mulled
iota
self-prophecy
alterations
abominations
flourish
sanctuary
unruly
predisposition
coincidence
sloughed
etching
apparition
whorl
insecurities
trauma

Discussion Questions

1. What are most people's first opinions of Owen? Are they usually accurate? (*Most people assume that Owen isn't smart because of his physical handicaps. On the contrary, though, Owen gets the best grades in his class.*)
2. Naomi thinks "the biggest problem" in her life is her name but that someday she will "live up to it" (p. 1). What does Gram tell her? Predict how you think Naomi will live up to her name. (*Gram says she is proud of their last name ["Outlaw"] and that there are worse things in life. She suggests that Naomi try not to embarrass the boys who tease her but instead concentrate on thinking positively. She suggests that Naomi start a new list titled "'Those boys* will not *bother me'" [p. 6]. Answers will vary.*)
3. Gram believes a person can make things happen by thinking "positive." Do you agree with Gram? What does Naomi say about thinking "positive"? (*Answers will vary. Naomi says positive thinking is "like magic," but it doesn't always work as she hopes.*)
4. Review the five items on Naomi's "Regular and Everyday Worries" list. Do you think any of the items are worth worrying about? (*Answers will vary.*)
5. Why does Gram call Naomi "brown shaggy dog"? Why does Owen call her "the center of a peanut butter sandwich between two pieces of white bread" (p. 11)? (*Gram says this because Naomi's hair is a "wild mop." Owen says this because Naomi takes after the Mexican side of the family and has brown eyes, hair, and skin. He and Gram, meanwhile, take after the Oklahoman side of the family and have fair skin and light-colored hair.*)
6. What do most folks say about Gram? Do you agree with them? How does Gram feel? (*Gram is Naomi and Owen's great-grandmother, so most people think she is too old to raise children. Answers will vary. Gram feels lucky to have Naomi and Owen and considers them prizes.*)
7. Why does Naomi carve soap and make lists? How do these activities help her? (*When Naomi first came to live with Gram, her hands shook and she didn't talk. Gram wanted to keep Naomi's mind and hands busy, so she introduced Naomi to the world of soap carving. Answers will vary but should include that soap carving and list making help Naomi sort through her worries and thoughts.*)

8. Why do you think Naomi is "never content" to carve just one of anything? (*Answers will vary. Suggestions: Two and three carvings may represent Naomi, Owen, and Gram. Wanting companionship for her carvings may represent Naomi's remembrance and/or fears of abandonment.*)
9. Why does Owen put tape on his shirt? Do you think Gram should make him remove the tape? (*for comfort and because it brings him a "peculiar satisfaction" [p. 20]; Answers will vary.*)
10. How do Gram, Naomi, and Owen feel about Skyla's sudden visit? (*Gram: looks as if she's seen a ghost, fears losing the children, protects Naomi and Owen and lets Skyla know she can't disrupt their lives, and angrily reminds Skyla of the children's past and how cruelly Skyla treated them. Naomi: vaguely remembers her mother's voice, eyes, and perfume, and feels queasy and worried yet can't wait to see Skyla again. Owen: "starry-eyed" and excited, and hopes Skyla missed them and wants to be involved in their lives.*)
11. How do Gram and Skyla recall the past differently? (*Gram says Skyla left Owen covered with infected insect bites and that Naomi refused to talk because of insecurities and other traumas. She says Skyla agreed when she abandoned the children not to interfere with Gram's raising them. Skyla makes light of the past and says Naomi was always stubborn and quiet, and Owen only had a few fleabites. She touts her parental rights and claims that it's time for her to get to know her children.*)
12. **Prediction:** How will Skyla's reappearance change life for Naomi, Owen, and Gram?

Supplementary Activities

1. Literary Analysis: Begin Character Attribute Webs (see p. 26 of this guide) for Naomi, Owen, Gram, and Skyla. Add to each chart as you read.
2. Literary Analysis: Begin the Story Map on page 27 of this guide. Add to it as you read.
3. Social Studies: Many families use a family tree to document their ancestors. However, Naomi and Owen belong to a non-traditional family, as they don't live with either of their parents. Design a family tree that would be useful for non-traditional families.
4. Art: Read "Soap Carving" at the back of the novel. Follow the instructions to create your own soap carving.

Chapters 3–5

Gram reminds Naomi and Owen about how their mother came to live with Gram before she married their father and how, after their divorce, Skyla left Naomi and Owen at Gram's apartment. Gram explains she doesn't have legal custody of the children. Naomi has never seen Gram so upset. Still, she and Owen look forward to fun, loving times with their mother. Skyla buys new clothes for Naomi but nothing for Owen. Before she leaves to meet her boyfriend, Skyla announces she will attend her children's upcoming teacher conferences.

Vocabulary
glorified
rehashing
defied
obligations
dervish
remnants
grating
conviction
catastrophe
shimmying
suspiciously
wriggling
riled
temperamental
recollection
deformed
awning
flitting
nimble

Discussion Questions

1. Why didn't Gram know Skyla until she was a teenager? Why does Gram say she couldn't do much with her? (*Skyla's mother got married and ran off to Kentucky. Skyla, who was then called Terri Lynn, came to live with Gram after her parents were killed in a car crash and her other grandparents didn't want her. By then, Skyla was too wild for Gram to handle.*)
2. Why did Naomi and Owen's parents divorce? (*They married young and had little in common. They weren't ready to raise children. Their plan to live in Mexico didn't work.*)
3. What does Naomi add to her "Things That [Are] the Good and the Bad All Rolled into One" list? What is good and what is bad about this addition? (*"Our mother came back" [p. 30]. Answers will vary. Suggestions: It would be good for the children to get to know their mother, and Skyla's return allows for this possibility. However, Skyla's presence also disrupts the children's lives and stirs their hopes of having a relationship with her. The consequences could be disastrous if Skyla deserts the children again.*)
4. Can Skyla take Naomi and Owen from Gram? Do you think the children should be with Gram or their mother? Explain any circumstances that may cause you to change your answer. (*Gram does not have a legal claim to Naomi and Owen even though she has raised them and has permission from Skyla to act as their guardian. Answers will vary. Discussion should cover the rights of everyone involved.*)
5. What does Naomi remember about her parents? Why do you think she has so few memories of them? (*Naomi doesn't remember her mother but has spent years imagining what her mother is like. She has one memory of her father. He rescued her and Owen during a storm and gave Naomi a carved elephant before he left and never returned. Answers will vary. Suggestions: Naomi's parents abandoned her at such a young age that she doesn't remember them. She subconsciously doesn't want to remember them because the memories are too painful.*)
6. Why doesn't Skyla match any of the mothers described on Naomi's "Possible Moms" list? (*Answers will vary but should include that the moms on Naomi's list make time for her. Skyla, meanwhile, abandoned Naomi and still seems more interested in her boyfriend than her children.*)
7. What information about her parents did Naomi pry from Gram? (*When the storm hit, Naomi and Owen's father was on a fishing trip. Naomi and Owen were supposed to be with their mother, but she'd left them alone to go shopping. A week later, Skyla left them with Gram, saying she couldn't handle two kids, especially with the added strain of Owen's physical disabilities.*)

8. Why does Naomi take out a family of elephants and put them on her shelf? Why do you think she chooses elephants? (*Naomi can't sleep, and she feels comfortable with the elephants guarding her. Answers will vary. Suggestion: To Naomi, elephants may represent security since her father gave her one during the storm.*)
9. What does Gram mean when she says, "'Let's...plant plenty of sunshine in our brains'" (p. 44)? What do Naomi and Owen hope will happen with their mother? (*Gram wants everyone to think positive and decides to give Skyla the benefit of the doubt. Naomi and Owen both imagine themselves spending quality time with Skyla, telling stories and catching up on their time apart. Naomi also wants Skyla to be proud of her and her soap carvings.*)
10. Why does Skyla shop for Naomi but not Owen? How does Skyla's attention affect Naomi? (*Skyla says it was a "shopping-for-the-girls day" [p. 47] and that she'll bring gifts for Owen next time. Naomi is thrilled to have new, store-bought clothes and lip gloss and is amazed when Skyla braids her hair. Skyla's comments cause Naomi to notice things about herself for the first time, like her heart-shaped face.*)
11. Skyla wants to attend Naomi's and Owen's teacher conferences, and Gram suggests that Skyla accompany Naomi and Owen in her place. What does this tell you about Skyla and Gram? (*Answers will vary. Suggestions: Skyla seems to be attempting to act like a responsible mother, though she leaves again and again to meet her boyfriend. Gram is considerate to offer Skyla time alone with the children.*)
12. **Prediction:** What will happen at the teacher conferences?

Supplementary Activities

1. Geography: Locate Rosarito Beach on a map of Mexico, and browse through a travel guide about the town. Discuss why Naomi's parents chose to live there.
2. Comprehension: Naomi has five items on her "Things That Were the Good and the Bad All Rolled into One" list. On a separate sheet of paper, explain the good and the bad of each item on Naomi's list. Then describe five things from your own life that are both good and bad.
3. Art: Review the author's description of Baby Beluga on page 30 of the novel. Make a diorama to illustrate Gram's trailer.
4. Math: Gram and Fabiola miss an episode of *Wheel of Fortune*, which ends their record at "743 during-the-week episodes" (p. 8). How many weeks in a row is this? How many years? (743 episodes ÷ 5 days in a week = 148 weeks + 3 days; 2 years and 10 months)
5. Science: Write a one-page report about hummingbirds and their territorial behavior. Include an illustration in your report.

Chapters 6–8

Naomi becomes friends with Blanca Paloma, a new girl at school who is bilingual and whose parents are also divorced. The girls arrange for their mothers to meet at the teacher conferences. On the day of the conferences, Owen wears his too-small best suit, with plenty of tape, and is teased by the kids at school. He refuses to blame the bullies, which frustrates Naomi.

At five o'clock, Naomi's teacher finds Naomi and Owen, still waiting for Skyla, who never comes. Naomi overhears her teacher tell the principal that Skyla has had problems with alcohol abuse and that Naomi and Owen's father had wanted custody of her and Owen, but Skyla refused. Naomi confronts Gram, who fills in more about the past and explains that Naomi and Owen's father sends money for their care but avoids contact. Gram admits she has kept this information from Naomi and Owen because she loves and doesn't want to lose them.

Three days later, Skyla returns and doesn't understand why everyone is upset with her. She announces that her boyfriend, Clive, will be a guest at Thanksgiving and then gives Owen a new bicycle. Skyla tells Naomi she expects her to thank Clive—loud and clear—for all her new things. She says Naomi owes him.

Vocabulary

plaited
ambience
sported
dapper
straggle
pitiful
rumpled
hoisted
irrational
dispensers
stock-still
dredge
deliberately
alcoholism
cattywampus
bluster
shenanigans
nettles

Discussion Questions

1. Why do you think Naomi and Blanca become friends so quickly? (*Answers will vary. Suggestions: The girls are opposites in their personalities—Naomi doesn't talk much, and Blanca is a "jabber-mouth"—but they also have a lot in common: divorced parents, Mexican ancestry, no other friends, etc.*)
2. How does Skyla treat Naomi and Owen differently? Why doesn't she treat them the same? (*Skyla buys things for Naomi but not Owen. She takes an interest in Naomi's appearance and is friendly to her but mostly ignores Owen. Answers will vary. Discussion could include when parents should and should not treat children the same.*)
3. When Skyla wakes up in a foul mood on the morning of the teacher conferences, how do Naomi and Owen react? What does this tell you about them? (*Naomi sits still, tries to please Skyla, and hopes Skyla's mood will change. She is relieved when things seem to get "back on track." Owen wears extra tape. Answers will vary but should include that Naomi and Owen are uncomfortable with—and almost fearful of—Skyla.*)
4. Why does Owen's ability to "look on the good side of everything" bother Naomi (p. 69)? Why do you think Owen has such a positive outlook? (*Naomi cares what other kids think about her and Owen. Answers will vary. Suggestion: Owen has adopted Gram's positive outlook.*)
5. What does Naomi learn about her parents when she overhears Ms. Morimoto and Ms. Domínguez's conversation? (*Skyla has a problem with alcohol abuse, has been in and out of rehab hospitals and halfway houses, and takes medication for related mood changes. Naomi and Owen's father wanted custody of the children, but Skyla wouldn't allow it.*)

6. Why is Gram "tight-lipped" about Naomi and Owen's parents? Do you think she is right to keep secrets from the children? (*Answers will vary. Suggestions: Gram wants Naomi and Owen to focus on the future. She wants to give Skyla a chance to build a relationship with them. She doesn't think their father's lifestyle was conducive to raising kids. She loves Naomi and Owen and doesn't want to lose them.*)
7. Why didn't Skyla come to the teacher conferences? How does she react when Gram confronts her? (*Skyla and Clive went to Palm Springs for a long weekend. Skyla doesn't understand why it is a big deal for her to have missed the conferences. She turns the situation around and says that Gram is "'raining on all of [her] joy'" [p. 84].*)
8. Naomi wants to hug Skyla for giving Owen the bicycle. What should have been a happy moment isn't. Why not? (*Skyla stands with her arms crossed and doesn't invite affection. When Naomi whispers a thank you, Skyla criticizes her and tells her to speak up. Then Skyla explains how she expects Naomi to act when Clive visits. She says Naomi owes Clive for all the things he's bought her.*)
9. **Prediction:** What will happen when Naomi meets Clive?

Supplementary Activities

1. Comprehension: Blanca says Naomi deserves to know about her life and that if Naomi asks a lot of questions, she'll get a lot of answers. On a separate sheet of paper, list questions you have about your parents and your past.
2. Art: Mr. Marble displays items collected by students and teachers. Make a display case for your classroom, and display items from different students each week.
3. Geography: Naomi adds Kalamazoo to her "Unusual Names" list. Work with a partner to locate 24 places with unusual names on a map or in an atlas. Then design a game of checkers from construction paper or other materials. Include the names of the places on the playing pieces and information about the places on the gameboard. Play checkers.
4. Science: Owen plans to show Skyla his "science potato" during teacher conferences. Make your own "science potato" by creating a potato maze. You will need:

   1 shoebox
   2 cardboard partitions (same width as short sides of shoebox)
   1 sprouting potato (leave potato at room temperature for six weeks to sprout)
   1 pot filled with damp potting soil
   tape
   scissors

   Plant the potato in the pot with most of the sprouts facing up. Cut a two-inch hole in one short side of the shoebox and in both cardboard partitions. Tape the cardboard partitions in the shoebox. Stagger placement of the three holes. Put the potted potato in the section farthest away from the hole in the shoebox. Close the shoebox, then place it near a window with the hole facing the light. Check the pot every day and water if the soil is dry. Record your observations as your "science potato" grows. Report your findings to the class.
5. Critical Thinking: Research factors that influence people to become bullies. Create a profile of Dustin Mullholler, the boy who bullies Owen. Explain why Dustin acts the way he does based on information from your profile.

Chapters 9–10

Skyla and Clive continue their selfish, greedy behavior during Thanksgiving dinner. Clive talks about his daughter Elizabeth, whom he has renamed Sapphire. Skyla tells Naomi she can watch over Sapphire when they move to Las Vegas. Clive upsets Gram when he asks how much she receives in state supplements for the children. When Clive considers using Owen and his checker-playing skills to make money, Skyla agrees potential bettors wouldn't suspect a crippled boy of having brains. Clive uses Naomi's soap carving of a delicate bird, her best work yet, to wash his hands, and he barely acknowledges her "thank you" for his gifts. Naomi suspects that Skyla is drinking again, but Skyla tells her to mind her own business.

At Owen's medical checkup, Skyla doesn't listen to the doctors' encouraging reports. She refers to Owen as a "Blem," a store's name for flawed, discounted shoes. Clive calls to tell Skyla that they will leave on Saturday for Las Vegas, and Skyla refuses to bring Owen with them. When Naomi defies Skyla's commands, Skyla slaps Naomi across the face. Angry and terrified, Naomi grabs Owen and flees to Fabiola's house, where Gram is working.

Vocabulary

cornucopias
toting
obsessed
mobile
supplement
dependents
custody
smirking
caterwaul
pediatrics
orthopedics
radiology
colleague
juncture
adolescence
defects
potential
ailments
swaddled
humiliate

Discussion Questions

1. How can you tell Naomi is nervous about Thanksgiving? Why is she nervous? (*Naomi breathes irregularly and tries to find matching cloth napkins. She is nervous about meeting Clive because she doesn't want to disappoint Skyla.*)
2. Why do Skyla and Bernardo have different opinions about the radish festival, *La Noche de los Rábanos*? (*Skyla associates the festival with Naomi and Owen's father, who left her alone with the children during Christmas to attend the festival. Bernardo is proud of his heritage and the festival's traditions because the event occurs in his hometown.*)
3. Clive has changed both his girlfriend's and daughter's names. What does this tell you about him? What names do you think he might choose for Naomi and Owen? (*Clive chooses names he can enjoy. This indicates that he is selfish and likes to control others. Answers will vary.*)
4. Why does Clive say Sapphire's mother isn't responsible with the state's money? Do you see a flaw in his thinking? (*Clive says Sapphire's mother is irresponsible because she spends too much on Sapphire. Answers will vary but should include that the money should be spent on the dependent's care, while Clive thinks the money should be spent in other ways.*)
5. Describe Clive and Skyla's plan. What are their motives? (*to take Naomi and Sapphire to Las Vegas; Answers will vary but should include that they want to collect state money for both girls and want Naomi to take care of Sapphire.*)
6. Why do you think Gram doesn't receive money from the state for Naomi and Owen's care? (*Answers will vary. Suggestions: Gram is proud and doesn't want help from others. She lives on the income she earns. Gram also may not know help is available, or she may not want to contact the state for fear that Naomi and Owen could be taken from her. Further, Gram may assume that the state would refuse to help her financially since she is not Naomi and Owen's legal guardian.*)

7. What does Clive think about Owen's skills at playing checkers? What is Skyla's opinion? (*Clive thinks he could make a fortune by betting on Owen. Skyla agrees that people wouldn't guess Owen's intelligence by his looks and "weird habits."*)
8. Why doesn't Naomi tell Gram about the beer in Clive's car? (*Naomi doesn't want Gram to worry and doesn't want to accuse Skyla until she is sure that Skyla is drinking again. Naomi doesn't want to make Skyla mad.*)
9. What do you learn from the scene at Children's Hospital? (*Skyla is drinking again. She is embarrassed by Owen's handicaps and thinks he is a "Blem," or defective. Gram's positive attitude has affected Naomi and Owen and allows them to see Owen's problems as slight compared to other patients. Owen's progress pleases the doctors, who offer encouraging words about his future. Owen is healthy and has a wonderful outlook on life.*)
10. What reason does Skyla give for her decision to not take Owen to Las Vegas? What is the real reason Skyla plans to leave Owen behind? (*Skyla says Owen will stay to take care of Gram. Skyla doesn't want Owen. She "'never could handle that situation and...still can't'" [p. 118].*)
11. Why does Skyla say Naomi hasn't changed since she was little? How does Skyla plan to make Naomi change? (*Skyla says Naomi still looks at her as if she is scared and still defies her. Skyla hits Naomi and says she plans to teach Naomi how to mind. Skyla also threatens to harm Gram.*)
12. Explain "a schizophrenia of hawks," the title of Chapter 10. How does this relate to Naomi and Owen? (*Answers will vary. Suggestions: Skyla's behavior is irrational and unpredictable. Skyla grabs Naomi "like a hawk diving for a morsel of meat" [p. 122]. Clive and Skyla are like hunting hawks, waiting to collect state money for Naomi and Sapphire. Discussion should cover schizophrenia, a mental disorder that affects a person's behavior and emotions. Skyla's behavior, both past and present, is the source of Naomi's and Owen's insecurities. Her alcoholism results in unpredictable mood swings, which deeply affect the children. Note that Skyla's psychological and emotional abuse is most likely the reason Owen uses tape and Naomi talks softly and worries. The children are uncomfortable with Skyla and never know what will make her angry.*)
13. **Prediction:** Will Naomi go to Las Vegas?

Supplementary Activities

1. Art/Interview: Review the author's description of Lulu's introduction to Clive. Research online or interview a dog trainer or a veterinarian to find out the best way to meet a dog for the first time. Create a poster to display in class.
2. Science: Choose six locations in the United States, and research each location's average temperature during November. Make a chart to show your findings.
3. Art: Create a mobile that shows the meaning of the saying "two peas in a pod" (p. 101).
4. Creative Writing: Gram says that Lulu is "'*usually* a fair judge of folks'" (p. 105). Write a humorous story in which Lulu judges contestants at a "people show." Explain how she chooses the winning person.
5. Comprehension: Hospitals give Skyla "'the creeps,'" yet Naomi thinks "'lots of people get better in hospitals'" (p. 110). Write a one-page essay in which you discuss your opinion of hospitals. Explain why you feel the way you do.

Chapters 11–12

Skyla protests that Gram doesn't have legal custody of the children, but Gram refutes Skyla's request to hand over Naomi. During the night, Gram, Fabiola, and Bernardo hitch Baby Beluga to Bernardo's truck and head for Oaxaca City, Mexico. Gram plans to ask Naomi and Owen's father to help her gain custody of the children. Naomi wants to stay with Gram and Owen and pins her hopes on finding her father. In Oaxaca City, with Baby Beluga safely hidden in the backyard of Fabiola's sister, Naomi relaxes.

Vocabulary

planing
shorn
barricade
cooing
lam
guardianship
notarized
mediator
dwindled
smudged
antsy
mesa
mottled
barrio
rickety
jacaranda
maverick
translating
conspiring
pirouettes

Discussion Questions

1. How does Naomi attempt to comfort Owen when he asks why Skyla doesn't want him? Do you think Naomi succeeds? (*Naomi says Skyla only wants her so she can serve as a friend for Clive's daughter and so Skyla and Clive can collect money from the state. She says they are lucky because Gram and their father want them. Answers will vary but should include that Owen knows Skyla has never wanted him.*)
2. Why does Skyla insist that she can take Naomi? How does Gram respond? (*Skyla says Gram doesn't have legal custody of the children, that a police officer would force Gram to give Naomi to her, and that a court would never deny custody to a child's natural parent. Gram says that the wishes of the children's father should be considered, as well as Skyla's history, and refuses to turn over Naomi because of Skyla's drunkenness.*)
3. Why does Gram take Naomi and Owen to Mexico? Do you think she has the right to take the children? (*to protect Naomi from Skyla and to show them their Mexican ancestry; Answers will vary.*)
4. Where do Gram and Fabiola go on their "private errands"? What do they accomplish? How did Clive help Gram? (*to an attorney; Gram receives temporary guardianship of Naomi and Owen. Clive gave Gram the idea of getting free legal aid to support the children.*)
5. Why does Gram say that she "could be opening another can of worms" (p. 134)? (*Gram realizes she must go to court to keep Naomi. However, a judge could award custody to Skyla instead of Gram. Also, if Gram contacts Naomi and Owen's father, he might want custody of the children and try to take them from her.*)
6. Why is Santiago important to Gram's plans? (*As the children's father, Santiago has rights, and his wishes will be important to a judge. Gram wants Santiago to write a letter to convince the judge not to give Naomi to Skyla.*)
7. Why does Naomi say her life is a "fog of the good and the bad" (p. 137)? (*Answers will vary. Suggestions: Naomi now has both good and bad memories of her mother. Her life is unsettled because she doesn't know if Skyla will take her and she doesn't know what to expect from her father.*)
8. Why does Flora and Pedro's yard make Naomi feel safe? (*It's "homey, like a trailer park" [p. 145], hidden from the street, and Skyla and Clive won't be able to find her there.*)

9. What happens to Gram's positive attitude? Why? (*Answers will vary. Suggestions: Gram worries that Naomi will be taken from her. She doesn't know if she will be able to find Santiago.*)
10. Why is Bernardo's art different when he is in Oaxaca? How can a place affect an artist's work? (*Bernardo calls Oaxaca "'a city of magic and surprises'" [p. 153]. He says that he is different when he visits Oaxaca and thus so is his art. Answers will vary.*)
11. **Prediction:** Who will find Santiago? How will he react?

Supplementary Activities

1. Health: Create an earthquake preparedness video. Show what to do before, during, and after an earthquake.
2. Geography: Lemon Tree is close to Tijuana. On a map of Mexico, locate Tijuana and Oaxaca City. Draw the route that Naomi travels from Tijuana to Oaxaca City. Add photos of interesting places along the route.
3. Science: Write a one-page report about the Mexican redknee tarantula. Include an illustration in your report.

Chapters 13–15

As the search for Santiago begins, Gram worries that Skyla will discover she took the children out of the United States. Naomi, Owen, and Rubén call names in the phone book to ask for information about Santiago. Though they get into trouble for making toll calls, they find Naomi's great aunt. Aunt Teresa gives Naomi a picture of her father, shows her his wood carvings, and says Santiago likely will be at *La Noche de los Rábanos* because a León has carved at the radish festival every year for over 100 years. However, Santiago doesn't arrive by the registration date for the festival, and he misses *Las Posadas*, a Christmas tradition he loves. Naomi arranges her soap figures on a tree branch and imagines the carving her father once made for her.

Vocabulary
gawking
deviated
chiles
recognition
destiny
traipsed
technically
pell-mell
animated
buffing
migration
ramshackle
brigade
participants
whittled
frustrations
procession
peppering
sapling
spindly

Discussion Questions

1. How is el mercado different from the grocery store Naomi had expected? (*El mercado is in a large building crowded with stalls and tables filled with everything from food to fireworks. Naomi describes it as "a party of colors and smells" [p. 155].*)
2. Beni angrily walks away from Bernardo and Pedro, but then returns and acts as if nothing has happened. What does this tell you about the characters? (*Answers will vary. Suggestions: The men have good relationships with each other and don't want to ruin them. They are stubborn, but they respect each other.*)
3. How does Naomi suggest that they find her father? How would you search for Santiago? (*Naomi suggests that they look in the phone book and talk to Bernardo's friends who knew Santiago. Answers will vary.*)
4. How does Gram act differently? Do you think she has forgotten what could happen to Naomi if they don't find Santiago? (*Gram isn't thinking positive. Answers will vary but should include that Gram has not forgotten what might happen to Naomi.*)

5. What does Skyla know that worries Gram? Why does this worry Gram? (*Skyla knows about the radish festival. Skyla may realize Gram took Naomi and Owen to Mexico, and Gram isn't supposed to take the children out of the United States.*)
6. Naomi suspects Gram would not let her call people listed in the phone book so she intends to keep the calls a secret. What does this tell you about Naomi? Do you think she disobeys Gram often? (*Answers will vary but should include that Naomi thinks finding Santiago is worth the risk of getting into trouble with Gram. Gram is surprised at Naomi's actions, which indicates Naomi doesn't disobey often.*)
7. Why does Graciela look worried when Rubén receives a phone call with good news? Why does Graciela smile when she turns around to make the call? (*Answers will vary. Suggestions: Graciela is worried about the cost of the toll calls. She may also be worried about her child's safety, since Rubén gave out his name and phone number to strangers in the phone book. She smiles because she is pleased that Gram will pay for the calls and discipline the children for making toll calls without permission. She also may be secretly proud of what the children accomplished by choosing to disobey her rules.*)
8. Why is Naomi proud to be a member of the León family? Do you know any families who are proud for a similar reason? (*The Leóns have been carving in the festival for over 100 years. Answers will vary.*)
9. Why does Naomi compare *Las Posadas* to her search for Santiago? (*Participants in the festival repeatedly knock on doors to seek shelter but are turned away. Similarly, Naomi continues to question people for information as to her father's whereabouts but always winds up facing a dead end.*)
10. Naomi pretends Graciela is her mother. Why would Naomi want Graciela as a mother? How is Graciela different from Skyla? (*Answers will vary. Suggestions: Naomi longs for a big family with a loving mother. Even though Graciela is separated from Rubén's father, she is very caring and would never leave her son. Skyla puts herself and what she wants ahead of her children.*)
11. **Prediction:** What will Beni, Bernardo, and Pedro carve for the festival?

Supplementary Activities

1. Geography: Naomi's father lives in Puerto Escondido, Mexico, which means "hidden port" in Spanish. Examine a map of California. On a separate sheet of paper, list ten places with Spanish names. Research the meaning of each name, and record your findings next to the corresponding word on your paper.
2. Science: The National Mexican Turtle Center, or *Centro Mexicano de la Tortuga,* is located near Puerto Escondido. Research the kinds of sea turtles found in Mexico. Create a poster that shows sea turtles' migration ashore to lay eggs. Include natural and man-made obstacles the turtles have to overcome.
3. Art: Read "My Journey to the Night of the Radishes" at the back of the novel. View pictures of radish carvings on the author's web site (www.pammunozryan.com/naomi.html [active at time of publication]). Sketch five radish carving ideas for Bernardo, Beni, and Pedro to enter in the festival. Choose the idea you would enter, and explain your choice.
4. Social Studies: Write a one-page report about the history of piñatas. Include step-by-step instructions that explain how to make a piñata. Create a piñata for your class.

Chapters 16–18

After Bernardo, Beni, and Pedro see Naomi's carvings decorating the tree branch, they decide on a similar design for their entry in the radish festival. They honor Naomi by asking her to carve a lion to top their entry. At the radish festival, Naomi can't find her father, and she and Gram worry that time is running out. Bernardo, Beni, and Pedro are announced as the second-place winners of the radish festival. Suddenly, Santiago appears to congratulate Bernardo. When he sees Naomi and Owen, however, he runs away, and Naomi chases after him. Later, Santiago arrives at the house and embraces his children in a loving moment that Naomi wishes would never end. Santiago's sadness over the "broken" family tradition that has endured for a century turns to pride when he looks at Naomi's lion carving and realizes that a León did, in fact, carve in the radish festival.

Vocabulary

trivet
contorted
anticipation
tainted
conclusion
tweaks
manicured
downhearted
sprawling
lounged
dramatic
extraordinary
compelling
commemorative
gazebo
terra-cotta
shards
instinctively
jabbering
revel

Discussion Questions

1. The author doesn't state how Naomi feels when the men decide to use her idea for their entry in the radish festival. How do you think Naomi feels? Are there any clues in the text to support your answer? (*Answers will vary but should include that Naomi likely feels pleased and proud. When Fabiola says the carving will be maravilloso, wonderful, Naomi plans to add the word to her "Superb Spanish Words" list.*)
2. How do Gram's and Bernardo's feelings differ about the radish carvings' disposal? Why do you think Gram's and Bernardo's opinions are so different? (*Gram thinks that the carvings don't last very long for all the work it takes to create them. Bernardo enjoys the work and participating in the festival. Answers will vary. Suggestions: Gram is an outsider. Bernardo is proud of the tradition.*)
3. What is the "tiny thread of hope" to which Naomi clings (p. 194)? Why does her radish carving make her think of this? (*Answers will vary but should include finding her father. She is carving a lion, or el león, which reminds her of her father's last name.*)
4. Why is Gram concerned with "practical matters"? (*Gram wonders if Skyla is right that a judge won't separate a natural mother from her child. She thinks she should prepare Naomi in case Naomi must live with Skyla or Santiago wants Naomi and Owen to live with him.*)
5. Why do so many carving contestants know Santiago? (*Answers will vary but should include that the festival participants are carvers, and the carving community is close. Also, Santiago comes from a famous family of carvers.*)
6. Why does Gram get "a bee in her bonnet" (p. 204)? What does Fabiola mean when she says that there were always politics involved? (*Gram thinks Bernardo, Beni, and Pedro's entry is better than the winning entry. Answers will vary. Discussion should include how "politics" affect judging and what other judged events are affected by "politics."*)
7. Do you think Santiago would have stopped running if Naomi had called him? Would he be more likely to respond to "Father" or "Santiago"? (*Answers will vary.*)

8. Naomi wants to go to Santiago but feels as if she is "knee-deep in wet cement" (p. 212). Why do you think she freezes? (*Answers will vary. Suggestions: Naomi is overwhelmed by her emotions. She may need her father to come to her.*)
9. Santiago is sad as he listens to Naomi tell the story of why they are in Mexico. Why is he sad? What does he think? (*Answers will vary. Suggestions: He regrets the time he has missed with his children and imagines how things could have been different for all of them.*)
10. **Prediction:** Will Santiago ask Naomi and Owen to live with him?

Supplementary Activities

1. Literary Analysis: Begin a Character Attribute Web (see p. 26 of this guide) for Santiago. Add to it as you read.
2. Writing: Santiago runs into the crowd when he sees Gram, Naomi, and Owen. Imagine you are Santiago. Write a journal entry about what you are thinking as you run away.
3. Health: Dried grasshoppers, called *chapulines*, are a treat in Oaxaca. Research the nutritional value of grasshoppers and other insects. Then compare the nutritional values of insects to beef, chicken, and fish. Summarize your findings in a chart.
4. Recipes: Make Mexican sandwiches. Serve with fresh fruit and *buñuelos* (recipe at back of novel).

   Tortas (Mexican sandwiches)
   soft French rolls
   cooked shredded chicken (or beef)
   refried beans
   grated cheese
   mashed avocado
   Optional ingredients: salsa, sour cream, shredded lettuce, tomato slices, chopped green chiles

   Slice the rolls in half. Spread refried beans onto bottom halves of rolls. Sprinkle with cheese. Spoon on shredded chicken. Add optional ingredients, if desired. Spread mashed avocado onto top halves of rolls. Place tops of rolls on *tortas*.
5. Personal Narrative: Naomi wants to remember everything about the night she found her father and feels as if she is in a movie she never wants to end. On a separate sheet of paper, write about a time you didn't want to end. Describe the memory in detail as though it were a scene from a movie.
6. Critical Thinking: Naomi makes *fantástico* the number one word on her "Superb Spanish Words" list. On a separate sheet of paper, list ten Spanish words that you think are superb. You may use a Spanish/English dictionary or a translation site on the Internet.

Chapter 19–a murmuration of tomorrows

Santiago teaches Naomi about her heritage and about carving. When Gram announces that they must soon return to Lemon Tree for the court hearing, Naomi begs to stay in Mexico. Santiago encourages her to be brave.

In court, the judge asks Naomi to explain any reasons she should not be with her mother. At first, Naomi can't speak. As she remembers her father's inspirational words, however, she gains enough courage to tell the truth about Skyla. When the judge learns Skyla doesn't want Owen, the judge decides to grant guardianship to Gram rather than separate Naomi and Owen.

At school, Mr. Marble and Blanca see changes in Naomi; she is no longer a mouse, but a lioness, and her voice is louder. Just as carving brings out what is inside wood or soap, Naomi realizes she is becoming the person she is meant to be.

Vocabulary

copal
intentions
machete
innards
chaffed
contracted
enlisting
rehabilitation
comprehensive
recommendation
commending
visitation
contemporary
refrains
sensation
clarified
flustered
entirety
ecstatic
countenance

Discussion Questions

1. Why do you think Santiago decorated the jacaranda tree with his animal carvings? (*Answers will vary. Suggestions: to serve as a Christmas tree; to represent the mobile he made Naomi and Owen when they were young; because of its similarity to Bernardo, Beni, and Pedro's radish festival entry*)
2. What does Santiago teach Naomi about carving? How could you apply this lesson to something besides carving? (*Though each piece has a personality, sometimes it isn't obvious until later what is hidden inside the wood or soap. Mistakes aren't always bad; they can unveil the piece's true identity and create destiny. Answers will vary but should include that the lesson applies to people—that what is inside isn't always visible at first, and that the mistakes in our lives shape us to become the person each of us is meant to be.*)
3. Santiago tells Naomi he is sorry he didn't fight for her when she was little. He says, "If I had been stronger, maybe things could have been different, but maybe they would not have been so different.... How will we ever know?" (p. 222). Do you think Naomi's and Owen's lives would have been different if they had lived with their father? Explain your answer. (*Answers will vary. Suggestions: Naomi and Owen wouldn't have felt as though both parents abandoned them. They might have had fewer insecurities. They still would have been hurt by Skyla's actions. They would have known more about their Mexican heritage instead of the Oklahoman side of their family. They may not have known Gram as well or adopted her positive outlook. Owen may not have had the same quality of medical care. Naomi probably still would have been a carver.*)
4. Why can't Naomi stay in Mexico? Why can't Santiago leave Mexico? (*Naomi's life is in California, and Santiago's work is in Mexico. Both parties would need time to prepare to make different arrangements.*)
5. Santiago believes "everything will be the way it was meant to be" (p. 226). Do you agree? Do you think this applies to everything in life? Why or why not? (*Answers will vary.*)

6. What is the significance of Naomi speaking loudly to the judge? (*Answers will vary. Suggestions: The judge must be able to hear Naomi. Speaking loudly shows that Naomi is now confident in herself, which will allow her to display her true feelings without worrying what others will say and think. Her confidence also enables Naomi to follow her father's advice and speak out against injustice. She is discovering the lion inside herself.*)
7. Do you think the judge would have ruled in Skyla's favor if she had wanted both Naomi and Owen? Or do you think the judge changed her mind because of what Naomi said? Do you think it would be difficult to be a judge? (*Answers will vary.*)
8. The "leftover kids" in the library admire Naomi's carvings, and Mr. Marble asks to display them at Open House. Do you think "Naomi, the Lion" still thinks of herself as a "leftover kid"? (*Answers will vary.*)
9. Consider how Naomi's journey to Mexico has changed her. Do you think the journey changed Owen? What would make Owen stop wearing tape on his shirts? (*Answers will vary.*)
10. **Prediction:** Will Naomi ever live in Mexico? Why or why not?

Supplementary Activities

1. Writing: Imagine you are Naomi. Write a letter to Blanca in which you summarize how the trip to Mexico changed you.
2. Art: Santiago carves a lion-girl figure for Naomi. Think about why a lion girl is a good choice for Naomi. Design a figure for Santiago to carve that would be a good choice for Owen.
3. Comprehension: The judge receives notarized letters from Ms. Morimoto, Mr. Marble, Mrs. Maloney, Naomi's counselor, and two doctors at Children's Hospital. List what you think each person included in his/her letter.
4. Theme Synthesis: Read "Becoming an Artist: Tips from Pam Muñoz Ryan" at the back of the novel. Apply the tips to the novel's theme of becoming who you are meant to be. Revise the seven steps to help you discover yourself.

Post-reading Discussion Questions

1. Why is the novel titled *Becoming Naomi León*? Brainstorm other possible titles for the book. (*Naomi is becoming the person she is meant to be. Answers will vary.*)
2. Which chapter title do you think best describes the novel's story? Why? (*Answers will vary.*)
3. How would the story be different if Gram had not been able to find Santiago? What do you think she would have done to protect Naomi from Skyla? (*Answers will vary. Suggestions: Gram may have been ordered to give Naomi to Skyla, though she may have convinced the judge to see her side. Gram may have run away with Naomi and Owen to Mexico since Bernardo and Fabiola have family there.*)
4. Which of the following do you think affects Naomi the most: her mother's return, finding her father, or learning about her Mexican heritage? Explain your answer. (*Answers will vary. Suggestions: If her mother had not returned, Naomi would not have gone to Mexico to meet her father and/or learned about her heritage. If Naomi had not found her father, the judge may have awarded custody to Skyla. If Naomi had not learned about her Mexican heritage, she may not have become "Naomi, the Lion."*)
5. Imagine how Owen feels to know that his mother doesn't want him. What advice would you give him? What would you tell Skyla? (*Answers will vary.*)
6. What are the main themes of the novel? Explain which one you think is the most important and why. (*non-traditional families, physical handicaps, bicultural heritage, fitting in, abandonment, courage, triumph over adversity, discovering one's self; Answers will vary.*)
7. A symbol is a person, object, idea, or event that stands for something else, often an idea. Do you see any symbols in the novel? (*Answers will vary. Possibilities: The branches used to hold carved figures could represent family trees; also, the branches used for carving have a hidden figure inside, like the real Naomi hidden inside herself. That Naomi carves figures in twos and threes could represent her desire for a family. Naomi's hair is unruly, yet grows out as she grows.*)
8. Read "About the Author" and "Q&A with Pam Muñoz Ryan" at the end of the novel. If you met the author, what questions would you ask her? (*Answers will vary.*)
9. How do you think Naomi or her story would be different if she had been given another name? How does a name affect a person's identity? (*Answers will vary.*)
10. Did reading *Becoming Naomi León* give you ideas about how to become the person you're meant to be? (*Answers will vary.*)

Post-reading Extension Activities

Writing

1. Imagine you are Naomi or Owen. Write a speech about children's rights in custody cases.
2. Write three paragraphs in which you compare a character from the novel to a person you know.
3. List the alphabet in two columns on a piece of paper. Use as many letters of the alphabet as you can to create titles of future lists that Naomi might make.
4. Write a poem about non-traditional families.

Music

5. Compose a song about your favorite scene in the novel. Set your lyrics to the tune of one of your favorite songs.

Interviewing

6. Interview your classmates about the novel. Summarize their opinions in a graph.

Speaking

7. Organize a classroom debate. Choose teams to support the viewpoints of parents, grandparents, other guardians, and children involved in custody cases. Debate solutions that are fair to all sides.
8. Create a list of adjectives to describe the person you are or are meant to be. Cut the list into strips, and then tape them to your shirt. Explain your choices to the class.

Art

9. Illustrate a scene from *Becoming Naomi León*. Use a tree branch as the centerpiece for your artwork.
10. Research the kinds of pottery made in Oaxaca (e.g., black pottery, glazed pottery). Make a clay pinch pot or Mexican coil pot (instructions available on the Internet). Use glaze to create designs on your pottery.

Social Studies

11. Design a travel brochure or Web site that invites Americans to visit Oaxaca. Include a brief history of Oaxaca as well as places to see and things to do that would interest tourists.
12. Participate in a Day of the Potato festival similar to the Night of the Radishes. Choose categories, and then have classmates enter carvings made from potatoes. Have teachers judge the carvings. Take pictures, and send them with an article about your festival to a local newspaper.

Assessment for *Becoming Naomi León*

Assessment is an ongoing process. The following ten items can be completed during the novel study. Once finished, the student and teacher will check the work. Points may be added to indicate the level of understanding.

Name ______________________________ Date ______________

Student	Teacher	
______	______	1. Complete the Sociogram on page 28 of this guide.
______	______	2. Write an essay in which you compare and contrast Naomi and Owen. Describe the characteristics each shares with Skyla, Santiago, and Gram.
______	______	3. Complete the Understanding Values chart on page 29 of this guide.
______	______	4. Write a poem about the León family's carving tradition. Include why this tradition is important to Naomi.
______	______	5. Complete the Cause/Effect Map on page 30 of this guide.
______	______	6. Choose 20 nouns from the novel that are important to the story. Sort the nouns into the following categories: characters, places, themes, events, and things.
______	______	7. Complete the Five Senses Chart on page 31 of this guide.
______	______	8. Summarize what you think the author's goal was in writing the novel. Explain what the author did that made you reach your conclusion.
______	______	9. Write a book review of the novel. Include whether you would recommend the book to other readers, and explain why. Send the review to your local newspaper.
______	______	10. Review your Story Map, Character Webs, Prediction Chart, and other graphic organizers with a partner. Correct all quizzes, tests, and vocabulary activities.

Using Predictions

We all make predictions as we read—little guesses about what will happen next, how a conflict will be resolved, which details will be important to the plot, which details will help fill in our sense of a character. Students should be encouraged to predict, to make sensible guesses as they read the novel.

As students work on their predictions, these discussion questions can be used to guide them: What are some of the ways to predict? What is the process of a sophisticated reader's thinking and predicting? What clues does an author give to help us make predictions? Why are some predictions more likely to be accurate than others?

Create a chart for recording predictions. This could either be an individual or class activity. As each subsequent chapter is discussed, students can review and correct their previous predictions about plot and characters as necessary.

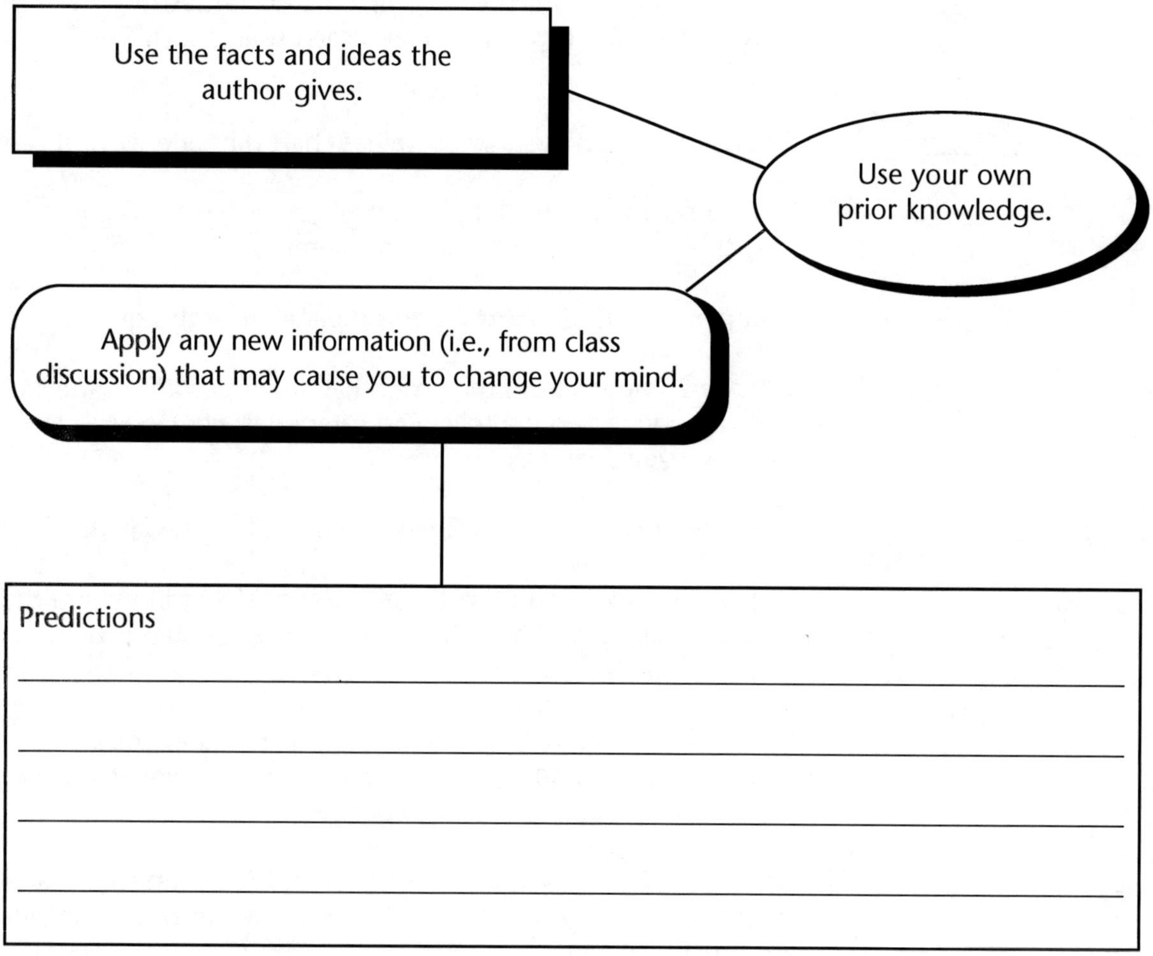

Use the facts and ideas the author gives.

Use your own prior knowledge.

Apply any new information (i.e., from class discussion) that may cause you to change your mind.

Predictions

____

____

____

____

Prediction Chart

What characters have you met so far?	What is the conflict in the story?	What are your predictions?	Why did you make these predictions?

Character Attribute Web

Directions: The attribute web below will help you gather clues the author provides about a character in the novel. Fill in the blanks with words and phrases that tell how the character acts and looks, as well as what the character says and feels.

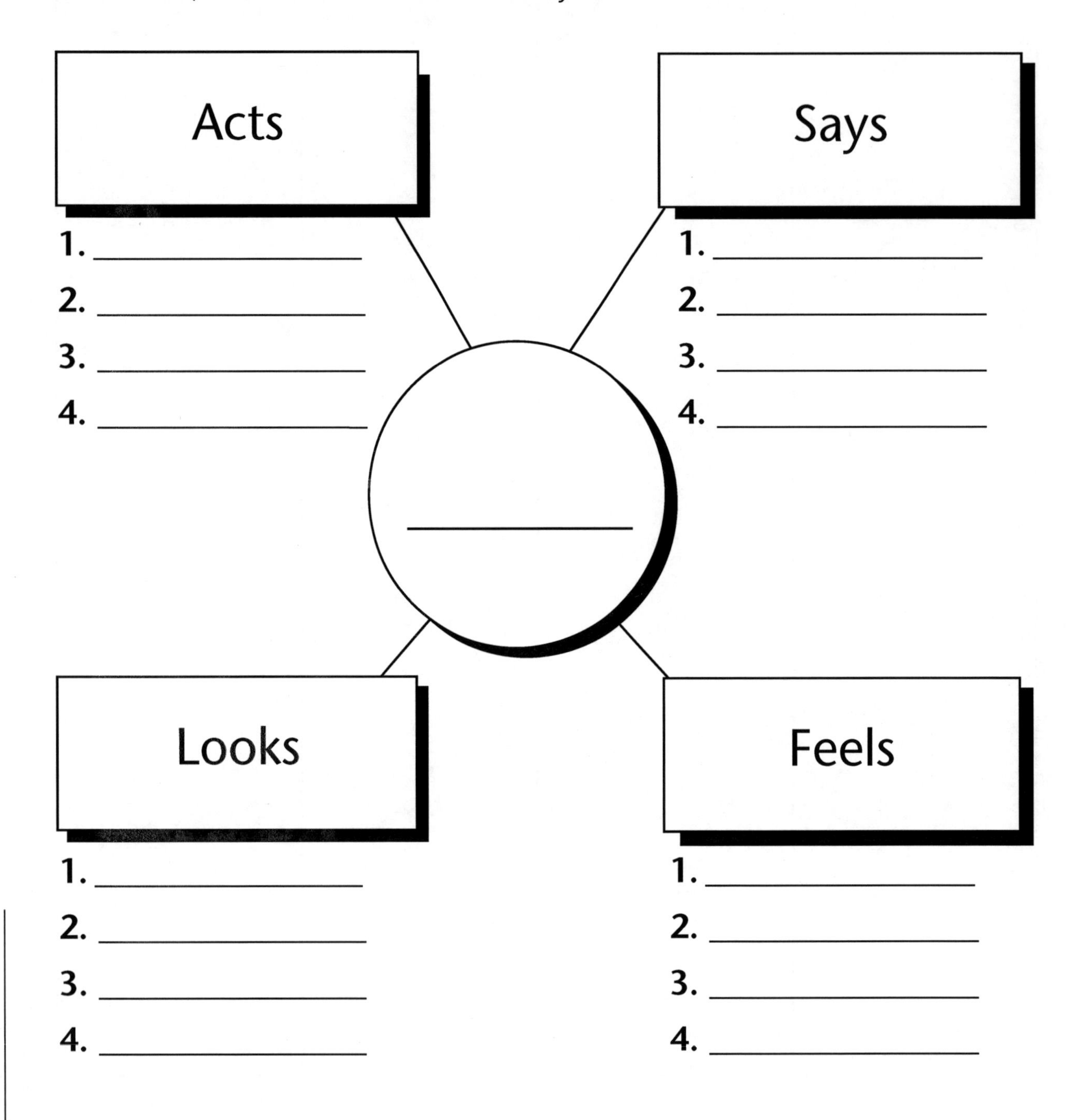

Story Map

Directions: Use information from the novel to complete the story map below.

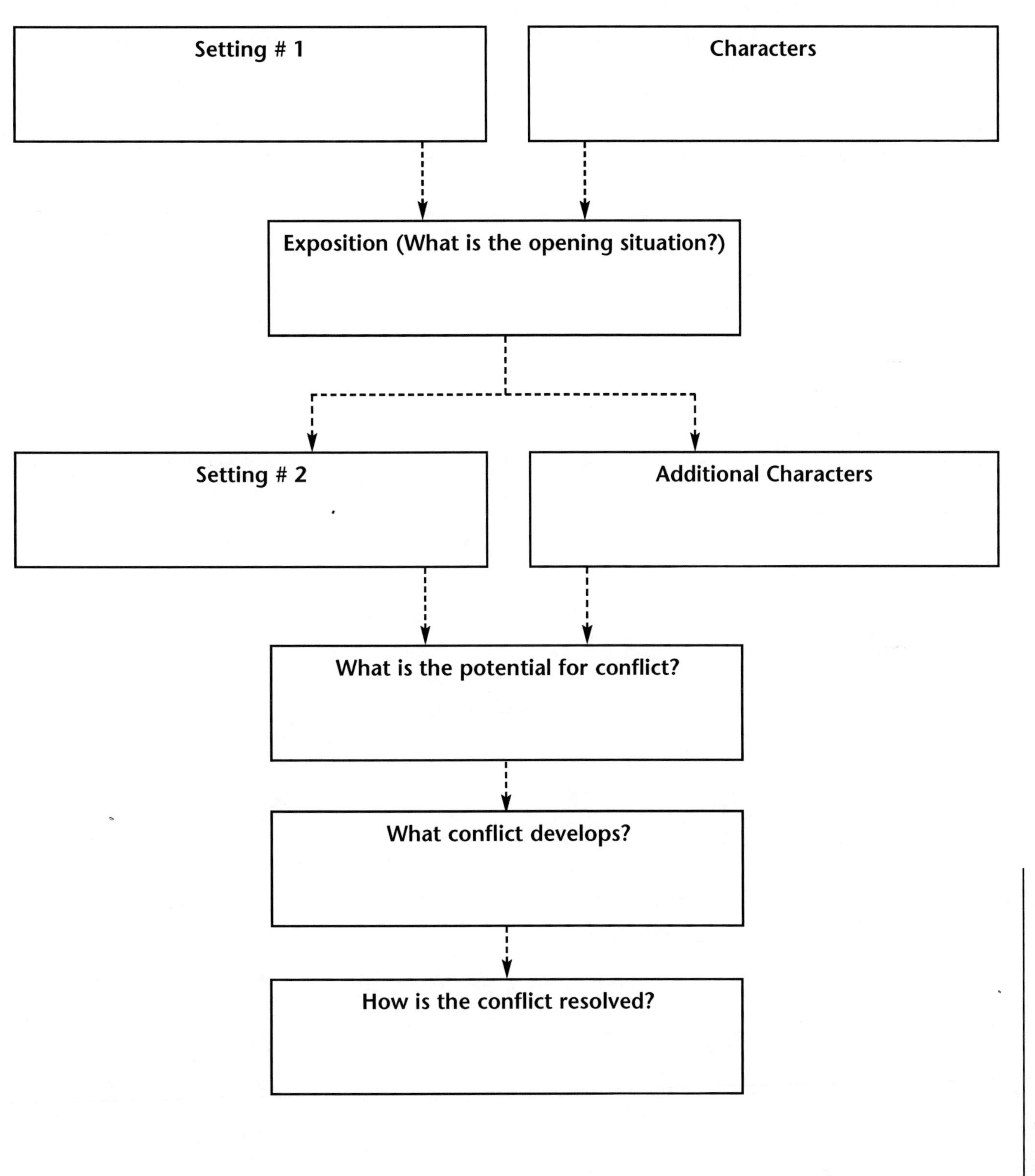

Sociogram

Directions: Write the name of a different character in each circle. On the "spokes" surrounding each character's name, write several adjectives that describe that character. How does one character influence another? On the arrows joining one character to another, write a description of the relationship between the two characters. Remember, relationships go both ways, so each line requires a descriptive word.

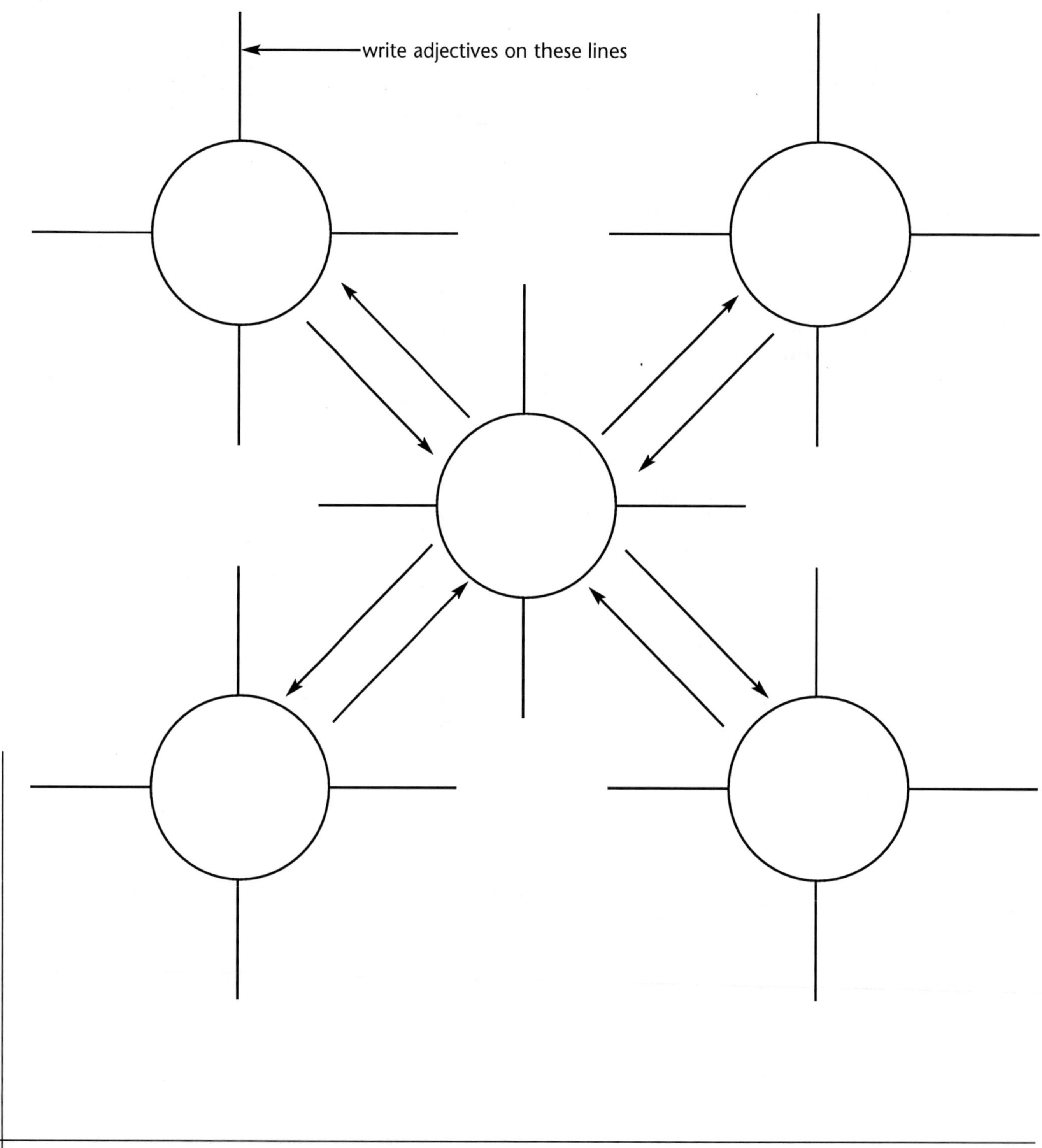

Understanding Values

Values represent people's beliefs about what is important, good, or worthwhile. For example, most families value spending time together.

Directions: Think about the following characters from the novel and the values they exhibit. What do they value? What beliefs do they have about what is important, good, or worthwhile? On the chart below, list each character's three most important values, from most important to least. Be prepared to share your lists during a class discussion.

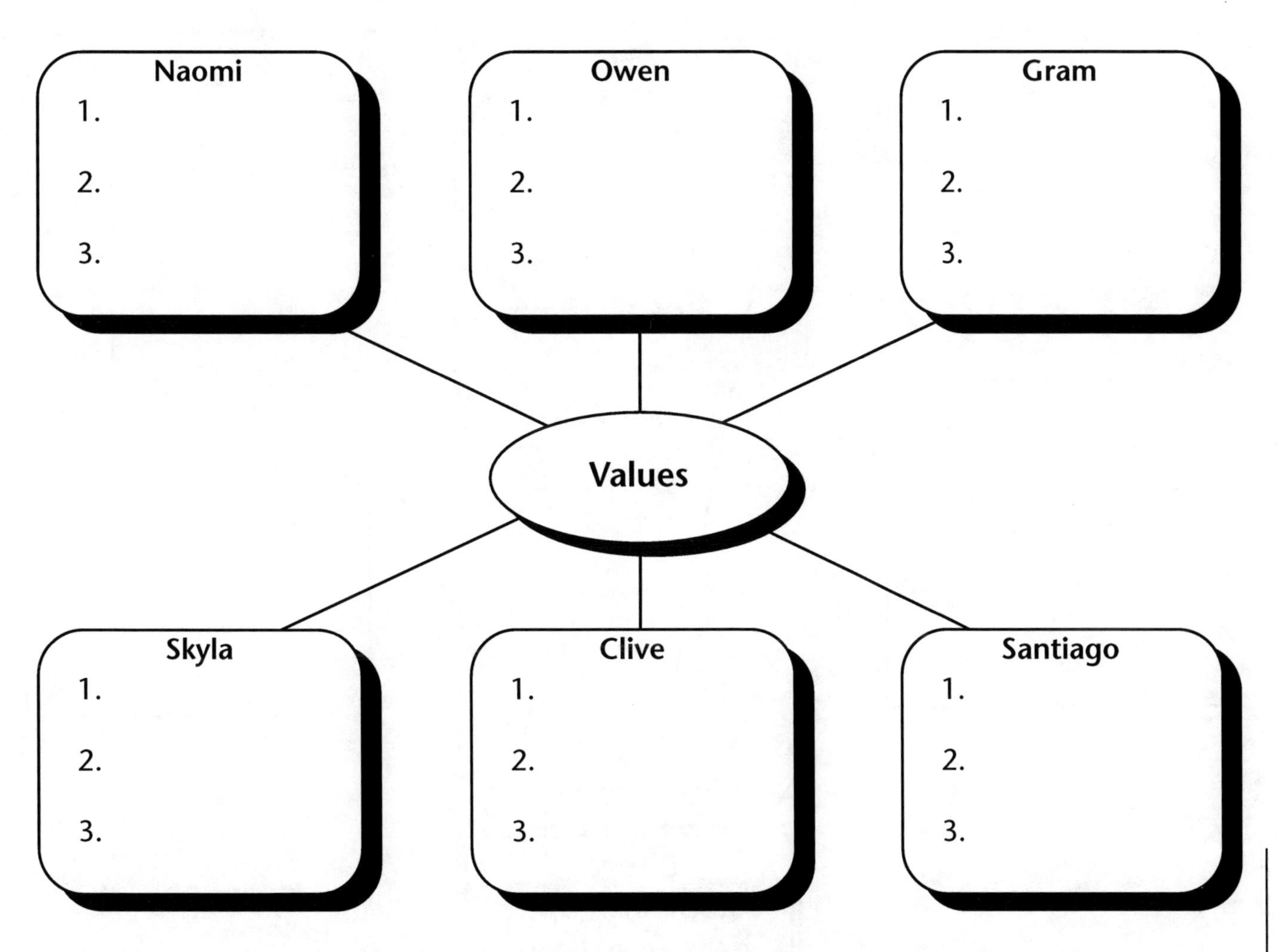

After you have finished the chart and participated in the class discussion, think about which character seems to have values most like your own. Write a paragraph that explains why you chose this character.

Cause/Effect Map

Directions: List events that cause Naomi to live up to her name. Write the events in the rectangles pointing to the effect.

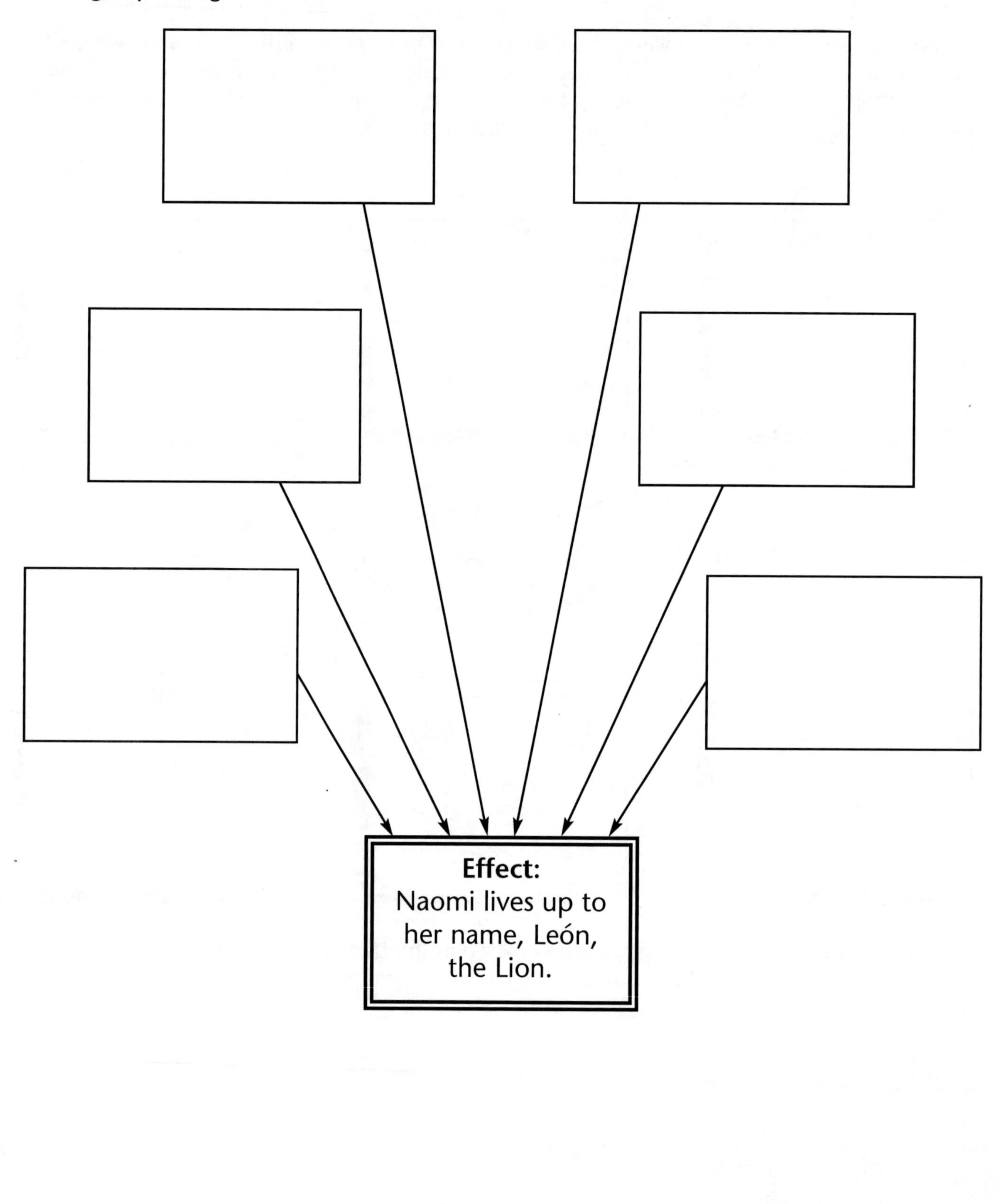

Five Senses Chart

Directions: List examples from the novel for each sense. Include the page number where you found the example.

Sight	Sounds	Touch	Taste	Smell

Linking Novel Units® Lessons to National and State Reading Assessments

During the past several years, an increasing number of students have faced some form of state-mandated competency testing in reading. Many states now administer state-developed assessments to measure the skills and knowledge emphasized in their particular reading curriculum. The discussion questions and post-reading questions in this Novel Units® Teacher Guide make excellent open-ended comprehension questions and may be used throughout the daily lessons as practice activities. The rubric below provides important information for evaluating responses to open-ended comprehension questions. Teachers may also use scoring rubrics provided for their own state's competency test.

Please note: The Novel Units® Student Packet contains optional open-ended questions in a format similar to many national and state reading assessments.

Scoring Rubric for Open-Ended Items

3-Exemplary	Thorough, complete ideas/information Clear organization throughout Logical reasoning/conclusions Thorough understanding of reading task Accurate, complete response
2-Sufficient	Many relevant ideas/pieces of information Clear organization throughout most of response Minor problems in logical reasoning/conclusions General understanding of reading task Generally accurate and complete response
1-Partially Sufficient	Minimally relevant ideas/information Obvious gaps in organization Obvious problems in logical reasoning/conclusions Minimal understanding of reading task Inaccuracies/incomplete response
0-Insufficient	Irrelevant ideas/information No coherent organization Major problems in logical reasoning/conclusions Little or no understanding of reading task Generally inaccurate/incomplete response